I0190179

A WALK THROUGH THE MEMORY PALACE

Pamela Johnson Parker

ISBN 978-0-9781749-6-5

All copyrights are retained by the original author and artist
(with the exception of online publication and
anthology rights by qarrtsiluni as publisher).

"Ulysses: Uxoria" (a section in "Archaic Fragments") was selected as
Switcheroo! poem of the month by *Broadsided*.
"Reading Keats in a Japanese Garden" was published
in *The Other Journal*.
"Breasts" was published in *New Madrid*.

Cover art: *Cupid Complaining to Venus,* by Carrie Ann Baade,
8" x 10", oil on copper, © 2005. www.carrieannbaade.com

Editors: Dave Bonta and Beth Adams
Design: ParcMedia.ca

Published by
qarrtsiluni
www.qarrtsiluni.com

in collaboration with

PHOENICIA PUBLISHING
MONTREAL

Table of Contents

78 RPM

Dusk and three minutes
Of fading light,
Pale as moonflowers,

Muted trumpets now,
Drawn up tight as those
Parasols propped in

The corner of your aunt's
Screened-in side porch, which
She calls *veranda*, where

White wicker bites
Through your white cotton
Shift, as she lifts a disk

Of black scratchy "wax,"
Places it on the Victrola,
Says, *I'll be back in*

A shake, you two, and
Disappears inside.
As the heavy arm angles

From left to right, as
The stylus traces
Its sapphire finger

Down the record's groove,
As he skates a single
Finger along the sun-

Bleached down of your
Arm, and as you
Start to shake,

Heart rising and
Falling like Billie's
Song, cool water poured

To the top, brimming,
Then spilling silver
Notes, and his lips

On yours for—
The stylus bumps
Its paste-paper

Center; you hear
The screen door's
Thump against its

Frame, hear Aunt's
High heels tick
Across the porch.

Here's something
For this heat,
She says, handing you

Each iced tea: beaded
Glass, mint and a
Paper umbrella

Blooming, a drink he
Grasps quickly and gulps.
You'll have to keep your

Knees pressed tight together.
As the light dims.
As the record changes.

TATTOOS

INK

Cardamom, ginger,
      pomegranate bark. Bamboo
         shoots, asparagus,

damp smouldering leaves—
      mugwort mordant in votives.
         Wicker baskets, rows

and rows of trays, jars
      decanting tarragon, dried
         dandelions, black

mushrooms, bear bladders.
      Aisles of densities, textures:
         dry dun-colored globes,

the testes of arctic
      seals; cicada skins, fingers
         of ginseng. Silver

Assam teas, great sacks
      of rice, geese screeching from crates.
         A string of small carved

jades by the cashbox—
      characters, crosses, one
         heart the size of a

thumbnail and grey-green,
      dark-veined, surprisingly rough.
         "Good for the kidneys,"

says the clerk—young, stripped
      to the waist, a great dragon's
         body rippling across

his back, undulant
      as he turns, wrapping spices,
         plum wine, packages

in brown kraft, tying
      them with string. Smoke from joss sticks
         swirls, that dragon's breath.

CANVAS

Sheets stiff as sacking;
    towels lacy from years of
        laundering; tables
pocked with cigarette
    burns; a ceiling fan wafting
        disinfectant, spent

passions; a slot machine
    dispensing condoms in three
        colors—red, navy, near-
black—*Stardust Hotel*
    Clean Rooms by the Hour—neon
        blues, reds, blurring past

our window, through blinds
    that won't quite shut (one slat slants
        diagonal) printing
its ladder of light
    all the way down your back. Here
        with you, I don't care

about tawdry or
    geography; I want you
        so much it hurts to
breathe, want your voice, telling
    me about anchors, hearts, names
        like *Winona*,

or *Felecia*
    (either regional or
        seductive); about
needles; about inks
    of cinnabar, navy, that
        almost piceous

black; about the tattoo
    of skin against skin, that
        most ephemeral
of canvases, which
    right now seems worth any
        multiplicity of stings.

FIRST ANNIVERSARY:
READING RUSSIAN LITERATURE

No money, so we sip from glass cups niched
In silver holders; I show you how my
Grandmother kept cubes of sugar between
Her teeth, *to make life sweeter*; I'm reading

Some dead poet (not *Zhivago*), tracing
Words—*samovar, nyet,* and the quicksilver
Cyrillic letters twining round the rust-
Dappled canister: Russian Caravan.

How our skin's slicked with sweat—too hot to
Sleep (or even stand); how all we can
Afford is this: back porch, spiked tea, spotting
These slugs. Each pair's a heat-slick valentine,

Drooping below the bleeding hearts you snitched
From a neighbor's garden—swollen pouts that
Blossom in shadow—and, like slugs, salt will
Melt them both. Sugar cube, teacup, mottled

Little leopards, milk-blue tin, pearls of heat,
Fringed branches, slow-swaying swing. You wish, like
A child at Christmas, for snow; *I loved you
Hopelessly* is all I remember of Pushkin.

(for Harvey)

ARCHAIC FRAGMENTS

NARCISSUS: NARKE

Water takes you in.
For days the gods talk
Of nothing but your

Spine in the dark, white
Coral, of how fish
School into your dead

Calm. And still water
Gives you back: thirsting,
Already bent to drink.

ULYSSES: UXORIA

Yes

After he told her
How he'd built their house around
That tree, after he

Described the dovetailed
Masonry, bole cut off right
At the root, leaving

One leafy branch as
Bedpost, after he reminded
Her he'd planed the wood

Yes

Till it curved, smooth as
Her hips, after he told her
How he'd laid in

Gold, silver, and strips
Of ivory pale as her
Skin, woven supple

Leather over its
Frame, oxhide gleaming red as
First blood—(that deerhound

I said

Pinning a weak-kneed
Fawn) and what one might call
First-blooded—given her

The *sema*, sign, their own
Life story, he asked, "Is my
Bed still there, or

Has another uprooted
That olive tree?" As she had
By now living proof,

Yes I will

She knew him again
And again, as the olive
Tree that's their rooted

Bed flowers fullest
In this, its second decade
As they delight in

Each other, as their
Sturdy bed blossoms in its
Continued cycle.

Yes

ENGENDERING: FOR TWO VOICES

I. PHEROMONES: GUIDEBOOK AND GIRL

Not all golden
but garish—mutations: vermillion;
pitch-black; vivid blue...

> I remember when
> I fed koi crumbled crackers,
> Cheerios, back

> in Baltimore, heard
> their mouths' *bob bob,* buoys above
> the water's surface.

Telescope eyes
bulge and pivot; diaphanous fins
drift in ribbons

> I was fifteen. A boy
> showed me his fish farm. Red
> hair fell over his

> forehead, glimmered
> over his freckled arms. Once
> I caught him blushing.

(curtains at an open
window); tiny gliders slice
like scythes through the shallows;

> He showed me graceful
> fantails, eye-popping Moors,
> calicoes, electric

> blue shubunkin. "Autumn
> brocade," he catalogued, "quick,
> not shy." Lionhead

blue indigo—
ink tattoos its tattering
stippling fintails;

veiltails, worth twice their
weight in gold, we fed with chopsticks.
"Put your fingers right

here, feel sandpaper
over the gills; males have it."
Helter-skelter, how

Narial's gills pulse
like twinned valves, celestial's
eyes are fixed firmly

we seined koi into
plastic bags. Gossamer veils
trailed from the dragonfish

he handed me; the weight
of the bag in my hand was
like holding a puddle.

toward heaven, mouth open,
choirboy holding the long
last note. He tells me

"Japanese keep these
in ceramic bowls, outdoor
pools. Viewed from above,

it's good for a fish
to have a skyward eye."
We both looked down until

a bubble-eye does headstands,
belly bumping, groping along
a floor it cannot see...

Ryukin's leap sent
him high over the water's
surface: *koinobori*,

low clouds, pond pocked with
rain, our fingers intertwined
and eyes still open.

II. PORTRAIT: MATISSE

I paint pictures, not
              women—as, when I say blue,
                            I never mean the sky…

These goldfish circling
              in their bowl (with its faint scent
                            of just-turned earth) are

curves she contemplates,
              chin to arm to chest, here in
                            his studio, still

before a quartet
              of faceless nudes smudged in one
                            corner, or the tapestry

of Persian-red curves,
              like the fish swirling in that
                            bowl, the brush curling

When I'm painting, I
              See how everything is
                            design: pure color,

on the palette, the arc
              of her shoulder…her expression blank
                            as the page before her—

she's going to write
              something, but what? Billowing
                            sails of the goldfish?

Chill of her skin as
              she poses still for him? Koi
                            back-stitched in heavy

brocade, there on that
              kimono she cast aside
                            while pillowing there?

The space occupied by
              the body, or the empty
                            space surrounding it…

III. POND: MIMESIS

Brass-yellow bubbler's
   eyes are marble-sized: water
      wings, fluid-filled

         First: spasmodic twitchings
           of tail; internal pulsations;
             irregular blobs

kidneys, scrotal pouches.
   Old goggle-eye, he cruises
      the mating pond, where

         of black and grey.
           newsprint. Four days: poppy seed
             eyes; the spine shows dark.

milling, gravid with
   eggs, females roil, here in
      the shallow murk, darting

         Five days: hatchling
           sloughs the silvery yolk, splits
             the soft husk in one

to mats of Spanish
   moss stacked like sofa pillows.
      Wriggling, shimmying,

         violent rending.
           Week's end: he begins the hasty
             search for shelter

forcing their way
   among the frenzied females,
      males bump, then curve

         among feathering
           fronds of sea fern. Ten days:
             baby koi flute through water

into pairs....Lulling,
    they retreat to deeper pools.
    The moss beads thick

swimming in an arc

with these orbs:

like punctuation

TAKING A WALK WITH YOU

"Walk forwards and backwards with me."
Kenneth Koch

Gazing into Wet
        Creek's tapestry, through
                the warp and weft of

minnows weaving
        in shafts of sunlight, echoed
                in the shadows of

the sawgrass swaying,
        in the small stream's undulance
                toward the river

torquing to the Ohio
        that somehow will spill
                into the Atlantic,

all salt spray hissing
        against rocks: the sound of
                repeatable longing.

That's there. And here a
        cardinal calls *Pretty*
                pretty pretty from

the pin oak, here a
        woodpecker strikes its match-
                head against old elm

bark, here the creek widens and
        narrows. Dear, the stents in
                your heart wend the same;

the plate and screws in my knees
        tell me before the skies do
                how there'll be rain, drops

canting crazily,
        pocking the creek. The bodies
                we have are also bodies

of water, bodies of dust, bodies
　　that change like clouds, bodies
　　　　that will fill, and fail,

and fall. *That's later.* Now as we thread
　　our way through cattails
　　　　in gauzy light, there's this

pause, an inrush of breath, holding
　　it, holding your hand
　　　　watching the water, the way

it flows, feeling my body moving
　　toward yours, as the water reflects us
　　　　as we were then , in its

mottled plane, *mirror,*
　　mirror, our younger
　　　　faces gazing back

at us from their side
　　of this day, as we work our
　　　　way, through cattails, through

muscadine, weaving through scything
　　sawgrass, sumac, taking the path
　　　　of least resistance.

UNREAL GARDENS WITHOUT TOADS IN THEM
OR, LAST YEAR'S JOURNAL, THIS YEAR'S YARD

Today's listless, nothing to
enumerate—no light
in its hues of jade, and no white-

green heads of hydrangea,
no dark hearts of redbud leaves,
no celadon of the sun-

lit maples, no sea-green treefrog's
back with each inclusion
of amber and topaz (*though he's*

never seen the sea, why
not sea-green?), no silver-tipped
spears of lavender now

poking up in the herbal bed—
only the sludge-brown creek
that borders the back fence is low,

going dry, khaki mud
on algaed stones usually
submerged. Not the way

I'd pictured it (*itinerant*
itinerary, sure)
but I'm listless, sketchy as

I sketch—no stepping-stones, no
new-legged tadpole, no minnow
(*Apostrophes? Commas?*);

no copperhead burnished in sun,
like hammered metal, like
sheet armor—only a shed skin

floating (*like a run in*
someone's stocking?) no tongue
forked out, flickering-only one

squat Buddha ignoring the sun,
the light, the list. Indolent.
What in my garden book I'd drawn

just last spring as fountains,
walkways, pools, are now fissures
pocked with gravel; the daylilies aren't

lowering their lemon-
butter heads, the willow's dreadlocks
aren't hung to dry in sun (*some girl*

hiding her face beneath
her heavy hair?)-No, it's really not
Appaloosa light, dawn,

late afternoon. I've copied out
You must change your life, and
really, I'm just too negligent

to care. The morning will spend itself
in a non-Eden such as this, where
only the sunlight seems lucid.

SOME YELLOW TULIPS

Old Mrs. Sonnenkratz, there in her yard
Bent over like a bulb herself, works hard

To edge her sidewalks, salt the slugs, and spray
The aphids from her roses. Every day

She's pruning, pulling, plucking, weeding out
The strays that might be festering. No doubt

She loves her lawn, loves order, symmetry
Of seedlings, herbal borders; she would be

Ruthless to seeds gone volunteer, to Queen
Anne's livid bruise, half-hidden in its green-

White froth of lace. Today, her turban slants
Askew over her blue-rinsed hair; her plants,

Once straight as soldiers on her patio,
Are *blitzkrieged* out of order, the yellow

Tulips (three days blossoming in a vase
Atop her wrought-iron table) don't erase

Her frown, her sloppy slippers, or the brown
Age spots (about the size of dimes around)

She often hides with gloves. A jagged scar
Runs up her forearm, where the numbers are.

The tulips, like her, blowsy, need to go;
Eine Kleine Nachtmusik's on her radio.

She thinks, *Acht nicht, acht nicht, nacht musik…*
Their leaves are lances, and they slant, oblique.

The tulips stems outlast their showy flowers;
For years she plants by day and, at night, cowers.

The yellow of the petals starts to burn;
Perhaps the worst of absence is return.

She smokes and shakes and smokes. Each flowerbed's
As neat as graves. She stubs out ash. The heads

Of these tulips wore bright turbans, tight-wrapped
And now unwrapping. In Berlin, she was slapped:

Sie ist ein Jude... Dry-eyed in Dachau, how
She's crying over bulbs bloomed too far now.

In a world of absence, presence leaves a scar.
Each tulip's ravelled to a six-point star.

(for Lilo Mueller)

READING KEATS IN A JAPANESE GARDEN

*"The bamboo plant, an essential element of Japanese painting, has
a life span of only a decade, dying when it flowers."*
                                    Little History of Landscape Painting

Stand of green bamboo:
        hollow-jointed flute whose leaves
                are lances; stems, turtles

cowering, shell to
        shell; blossoming white, world-wide,
                then gone, in one

superlative spring;
        o mother of paper, o father
                of pen, o teacher

of all we need know
        on earth—beauty's the greatest
                distance between faults.

BREASTS

Figure A.   Woman, nude from the waist up, standing in front
of mirror. Arms raised above head; breasts
inspected for dimpling, thickening.

Tin tub, hot water hauled
Steaming from the stove, steaming
The mirror. Lye soap.

Flare of hips, bare back,
Her hair slipping its awkward
Snood, rippling past her

Shoulders. Left arm crooked
Over head, that beautiful
Tilt, that supplication.

Sponging off the sweat
From packing pecans all day,
Culling the kernels

At Roper Candies,
Sponging under arms—downy
Hair iridescent

With suds, sponging
Under breasts. Looking down.
19. Nipple. Nipple.

Figure B.   Woman face up, flat in bed, small pillow under left
shoulder. Position prevents sagging, results in
satisfactory inspection.

Reading in bed, learning
The body the way the blind
Learn Braille, fingers against

Skin, scanning. Circling,
Circling from the shoulder inward
Inward. Fingers slick

With Jergens gliding
Over the breast—*water skate*
Skimming the thin skin

Of the pond—spiraling
     Inward like a nautilus,
         Stippled, thicker here.

39. Hackle. Hackle.

Figure C.   Recent radical mastectomy showing markings for
radiation. Incisions placed so that they will not show
when wearing evening dress or bathing suit.

Suturing, suturing,
     Interrupted silk. The scar
         Crosshatched, diagonal

From shoulder to her
     Xiphisternum. Zipper, zipper.
         Something's wrong with this

White leather, this
     Epidermis sliced and scraped
         And stitched—no nipple,

No tissue, no muscle,
     No lilt—skin stretched like canvas
         Over washboard ribs.

She can see straight down to
     Her pubis. It hurts to zip
         Her dress, brush her hair.

She used to be quite
     The seamstress, hands darting here and
         There. No pattern now.

49. Radical, radical.

Figure D.   Table showing statistical survey of definite
tendency toward the development of breast cancer
among family members.

Spring's sprung, I'm ten, I
     Don't ever want to get tits—
         I've seen my grandmother

Changing clothes, changing.
        She didn't know I was watching
                Her, watching. I'd gone

Outside, climbed up in
        The pear tree, its dark branches
                Weighed down with a pearly

Spray of bloom. I'd shaken
        Its limbs, bruised its thick clouds
                Of blossom, littered

The ground with petals.
        Pollen fell all over me,
                A layer of gold, gilding

Gilding. *Something's changed.*
        I can smell the sweet rot of
                Bloom, can hear the bees

Buzz as they suckle, see
        For the first time how each petal
                Isn't pure white but

Curled at each edge, pale brown.
        Some day I'll need a bra, some
                Day I'll sag like Gran.

Not me. Not now.

Figure E.   Pathologist inspecting each slide of fine needle
aspiration carefully for basal cell changes. His role
is vital in the preservation of the woman's breast.

My boyfriend at work:
        White walls, white rats, white lab coat,
                White hands adjusting

The lens. He works as
        A pathologist, sifting
                Through slides for changes

In cells, staining them
        Violet, murmuring words like
                Metastasis, like

Carcinoma. Low
      In the throat, almost purring.
            This is what it looks

Like; this is a textbook
      Case of CA, he says. And,
            Sometimes when I can't

Find anything, I
      Stay here half the night. I like
            To find it, like to

Find it. He's been my boyfriend
      For weeks now, lover, lover.
            He keeps telling me

You've got terrific lungs.

Figure F.   Mammogram showing stellate lesions, suspicious
for breast cancer. Note the clusters, in pairs.

Daughter, we're rocking
      And at my breast you tunnel,
            Tugging, tweaking, your

Little mewlings a pleasure
      As unexpected as this ringing.
            Whoever's calling

At 2 a.m., I'm
      Thinking of carnage. It's my
            Baby sister. *I have*

Stage IV, stage IV, and
      Can you come right out? Between
            Our phones, there's the roar

Like the ocean's, as
      If we were holding shells up
            To our ears, a song

Not unlike the blood's.
      She's only 40. *Tattoo.*
            Radiation markings.

Ablation. Neither
    Of us will say *cancer*,
        Neither of us

Mentions our mother.
    Daughter, I hold you tighter
        To my breast.

A Note on the Award

A Walk Through the Memory Palace, by Pamela Johnson Parker, was the first-place winner of *qarrtsiluni's* 2009 poetry chapbook contest, selected by Dinty Moore.

A Walk Through the Memory Palace was simultaneously published in electronic form at http://memorypalacewalk.com, as a downloadable audio file; and in this print edition, available through Amazon.com.

About the Author

Pamela Johnson Parker is a medical editor and adjunct professor in creative writing and poetry. Her poems, flash fiction, and essays have appeared in or are forthcoming in *qarrtsiluni, The Binnacle, The Other Journal, New Madrid, Pebble Lake Review, Holly Rose Review, Six Sentences, MiPOesias, Muscadine Lines: A Southern Journal,* and *Anti-*. She is also the featured poet in the April 2009 *Broadsided* series of poetry and art. A graduate of the MFA program at Murray State University, Parker lives in western Kentucky. She blogs at http://chisenbop.blogspot.com.

www.ingramcontent.com/pod-product-compliance
Lightning Source LLC
Chambersburg PA
CBHW060045040426
42331CB00032B/2433